MONUMENTAL MILESTONES
GREAT EVENTS OF MODERN TIMES

Desegregating America's Schools

An armed guard patrols Tennessee's Clinton High School to deter rioting when black students attend for the first time.

Mitchell Lane

PUBLISHERS
P.O. Box 196
Hockessin, Delaware 19707

Titles in the Series

Desegregating America's Schools

After the *Brown v. Board* decision was read in 1954, many people became angry. Some vowed that they would not allow schools in their communities to desegregate.

KaaVonia Hinton

PUBLISHERS

Printing   1   2   3   4   5   6   7   8   9

Library of Congress Cataloging-in-Publication Data
Hinton, KaaVonia, 1973–
  Desegregating America's schools / by KaaVonia Hinton.
      p. cm. — (Monumental milestones)
  Includes bibliographical references and index.
  ISBN 978-1-58415-737-3 (library bound)
  1. School integration—United States—History—Juvenile literature. 2. Segregation in education—United States—History—Juvenile literature. 3. Discrimination in education—United States—History—Juvenile literature. I. Title.
  LC214.2.H56 2010
  379.2'63—dc22

                                                                              2009027365

ABOUT THE AUTHOR: KaaVonia Hinton is the author of *Angela Johnson: Poetic Prose* (2006) and *Sharon M. Draper: Embracing Literacy* (2009). She is also coauthor (with Gail K. Dickinson) of *Integrating Multicultural Literature in Libraries and Classrooms in Secondary Schools* (2007) and (with Katherine T. Bucher) of *Young Adult Literature: Exploration, Evaluation, and Appreciation* (Prentice Hall, 2009). For Mitchell Lane Publishers, she has written *Jaqueline Woodson, Brown v. Board of Education of Topeka, Kansas, 1954,* and *The Story of the Underground Railroad*.

PUBLISHER'S NOTE: This story is based on the author's extensive research, which she believes to be accurate. Documentation of such research is contained on page 46.

The internet sites referenced herein were active as of the publication date. Due to the fleeting nature of some web sites, we cannot guarantee they will all be active when you are reading this book.

MONUMENTAL MILESTONES
GREAT EVENTS OF MODERN TIMES

Contents

*For Your Information

A bus station in Durham, North Carolina, had separate sections for blacks and whites.

In 1896, the Supreme Court ruled that segregation was legal. If blacks and whites were traveling together, they could not stay at the same hotel. They also used separate waiting rooms, water fountains, and bathrooms. They were even separated when they died; black and white people were buried in different cemeteries.

Separate and Unequal

Americans have always believed that education is the key to success. But they have disagreed about who should be educated. During slavery, it was against the law to teach slaves to read or write, because education is powerful. An educated slave might discover ways to free herself and others. Slaves knew the importance of education, so they found ways to create secret schools. After slavery ended, the number of opportunities for former slaves to become educated grew.

Right after the Civil War, in a period in history called Reconstruction, the United States government developed plans to help former slaves learn to read and write, get jobs, and enjoy the benefits of American citizenship. One helpful program the government put in place was the Freedmen's Bureau. While the Freedmen's Bureau created programs in all aspects of life, it had a great impact on education. It established free education for children and adults. The bureau also helped found some of the nation's historically African American colleges and universities, including Fisk University, Hampton University, and Howard University.

Some whites did not want African Americans to have the opportunity to become educated at all, while others insisted that if African Americans were to be educated, they should have their own schools. Many have felt that creating separate schools for African Americans is unfair. As early as the mid 1800s, lawsuits were filed to fight against segregation. Five-year-old Sarah C. Roberts of Boston, Massachusetts, was at the center of one of the first cases that argued against segregated schools. Since Sarah had to walk past five white schools to get to her all-black school, her father, Benjamin F. Roberts, sued the city of Boston. Roberts believed his daughter should attend the school closest to her home.

Despite the strong arguments of two lawyers, abolitionist Charles Sumner and Robert Morris, an important African American attorney, the Roberts family lost the case. Sumner and Morris insisted that separate schools could never be equal, but in 1850, Chief Justice Lemuel Shaw of the Massachusetts Supreme Judicial Court ruled that segregated schools were legal. However, a few years later, in 1855, Massachusetts schools were desegregated.

After Reconstruction ended in 1877 and the Freedmen's Bureau was closed, life for African Americans changed. Free schooling for African Americans in the South began to decrease. White teachers and missionaries who had educated African Americans during Reconstruction were forbidden to continue. The South became completely segregated. African Americans and whites had separate water fountains, seating areas, public rest rooms, and schools. An African American man named Homer Plessy, who looked white but had African American ancestors, decided to challenge segregation by sitting in the white section of a train in Louisiana. He was taken to jail and fined for breaking the law. In the court case *Plessy v. Ferguson*, the Supreme Court ruled once again that segregation was legal.

Just as the *Roberts v. The City of Boston* court ruling had done nearly fifty years earlier, *Plessy v. Ferguson* encouraged states to promote segregation. The state of Kentucky passed a law in 1904 that prohibited integrated education. Berea College, a private school that had always taught African Americans and whites, challenged the law in the Kentucky Court of Appeals and lost. The case was appealed to the United States Supreme Court, which ruled in 1908 that Kentucky had the right to prohibit integration. This case gave all states the right to insist on segregated education in private and public schools.

Laws stated that schools must be separate *and* equal. However, visits to African American and white schools in the same cities proved otherwise. Charles Hamilton Houston, the vice-dean of Howard University's Law School from 1929 until 1935, toured the South and created a film about the schools in South Carolina. The film was called *A Study of Educational Inequalities in South Carolina*.[1] Black schools often had outdoor toilets, leaky roofs, broken windows, and crowded classrooms, while white schools tended to have indoor plumbing and new books, equipment, and furniture.

With the help of the National Association for the Advancement of Colored People (NAACP), citizens who wanted blacks to have a better education began to sue school boards. Levi Pearson of South Carolina is one example. Since his children had to walk several miles to get to school, he asked the school board to provide a bus for the African American students, especially since the white schools had buses. The school board denied Pearson's request, arguing that African Americans did not pay enough taxes to afford buses for their schools. Pearson sued, but in the end, the African American community had to buy its own bus.

The NAACP believed it was important to use the law to fight for better conditions in African American schools. In 1915, the organization began hiring lawyers. By the 1930s, Nathan Margold had developed a plan that advised lawyers to challenge school segregation by proving that African American schools were not equal to white schools. Charles Houston altered the plan because he believed the NAACP would gain greater success if lawyers challenged segregation at the university level before attacking it in elementary and high schools. Houston chose many of the attorneys he trained at Howard University

It was a personal triumph for Marshall when he and Charles Houston convinced the Maryland Court of Appeals to order the University of Maryland Law School to admit Murray.

Thurgood Marshall (left) had just graduated from law school when he signed on to help Donald Murray (right) win his case.

to help him. One of the lawyers he chose was Thurgood Marshall, who was practicing law in Maryland at the time. Since Houston was looking for a case that would challenge segregated law schools, Marshall told Houston about Donald Gaines Murray.

Murray was not allowed to attend the University of Maryland Law School because he was African American. Houston and Marshall became Murray's lawyers. In court, they argued that Murray should be accepted because he was qualified. The judge agreed with Houston and Marshall and ruled that Murray be admitted to the all-white university. The success of the Murray case gave the NAACP and the African American community hope that segregated schools would become illegal.

Houston and Marshall worked successfully on several cases before Houston went to work in his father's law firm. Marshall took over and started the NAACP's Legal Defense and Educational Fund, which would help poor people with legal problems. By 1950, when courts in different states had begun to agree that separate but equal universities could not exist, Marshall held a conference with other lawyers so that they could plan how the NAACP would continue to challenge injustices in education. They decided to fight school segregation at the kindergarten through high school level. The NAACP looked for cases in different parts of the country that could be used to argue that separate schools could never be equal. They would be considered together in the case *Brown v. Board of Education of Topeka, Kansas.*

When Thurgood Marshall spoke to the judges in the Supreme Court during the *Brown v. Board of Education of Topeka, Kansas* trial, the judges reminded him that during the 1800s a similar case had come before the court. The case was *Roberts v. The City of Boston.*

Sarah Roberts' father asked the Primary School Committee of Boston, Massachusetts, if Sarah could attend the school closest to their home, but the committee said no because she was black and the closest school was for whites. Next, Roberts told the General School Committee that the Smith School was too far for Sarah to walk, especially since she passed five white schools on the way to the all-black school. Unmoved, the General School Committee told Roberts that despite Sarah's long walk, she still had to attend the Smith School.

Angry, Roberts decided to enroll Sarah at the Phillips School without permission from the committee, but Principal Andrew Cotton denied Sarah admission. Then Roberts tried to enroll her in the Otis School and was successful. When the school committee found out, they sent the police to remove Sarah from the Otis School. Roberts refused to send Sarah to the Smith School because he did not think segregated schools were fair.

In 1848, Roberts went to Robert Morris, an African American lawyer who by that time had argued only one case, and asked for help. Roberts told Morris he wanted him to help him get Sarah admitted in the school near her home. Roberts sued the city of Boston, but Morris lost the case. After appealing, Morris asked Charles Sumner, a more experienced lawyer, to help him argue the case in the Supreme Judicial Court of Massachusetts. Morris and Sumner lost the case, but five years later, schools in Boston were integrated, and Sarah Roberts was able to enroll in the school closest to her home.

OTIS SCHOOL, LANCASTER STREET.

Etching of Boston's Otis School from 1851

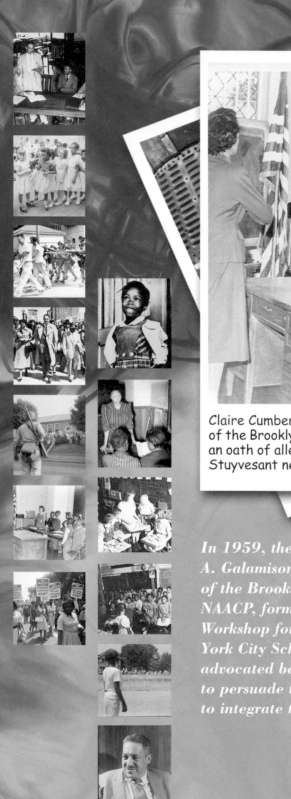

Claire Cumberbatch, community activist and a member of the Brooklyn, New York, branch of the NAACP, leads an oath of allegiance at a school in Brooklyn's Bedford-Stuyvesant neighborhood.

In 1959, the Reverend Milton A. Galamison, former president of the Brooklyn branch of the NAACP, formed the Parents' Workshop for Equality in New York City Schools. The group advocated boycotting schools to persuade the school board to integrate them.

Brown v. Board of Education of Topeka, Kansas

After careful planning, the NAACP lawyers decided that in upcoming court cases they would argue that the *Plessy v. Ferguson* ruling—which said separate-but-equal schools and other public facilities such as buses were legal—was wrong. The NAACP also planned to argue that separate-but-equal schools were actually illegal because the Fourteenth Amendment said all citizens should receive "equal protection under the laws."[1] If this argument did not work, they planned to prove schools could only be equal if they were desegregated.

With a definite plan in place, the NAACP turned its attention to Clarendon County in South Carolina. Schools were separate and unequal in that county. White schools received nearly three times more money per student than African American schools received. The African American schools also had fewer teachers. African American families were frustrated because they had already tried to get equal transportation and failed. Joseph Albert DeLaine, an African American minister and teacher, encouraged twenty parents to sue for desegregation rather than for equal transportation. The first person to sign the lawsuit was Harry Briggs, so the case, *Briggs v. Clarendon County, South Carolina*, is named after him.

The Briggs case was argued in court in 1951. Though Marshall argued passionately that segregation was unconstitutional, the judges did not agree, so Marshall appealed to the United States Supreme Court.

A few days later, the NAACP lawyers traveled to Topeka, Kansas. In Topeka, secondary schools were integrated, but elementary schools were not. Though the all-white Sumner School was close to her home, seven-year-old Linda Carol Brown had to "walk between . . . train tracks for half a dozen blocks" to get to her bus stop, which was seven blocks from her home.[2] Once on the bus, she traveled for thirty minutes to the all-black Monroe School. Just before Linda was to begin third grade, her father, the Reverend Oliver Brown, tried to enroll her in the Sumner School but was refused. The NAACP developed a lawsuit against the Board of Education of Topeka, Kansas, and Brown was the first to sign it. Brown and the others who signed the lawsuit lost the case, but the district court did agree that segregated schools were unequal.

Similarly, after hearing two court cases—*Belton v. Gebhart* and *Bulah v. Gebhart*—the court agreed that separate schools in Delaware were not equal. The judge ruled that African American students should be admitted to white elementary and high schools. This was the first call for integration at the elementary and secondary level.

The first case developed when African American students living in Claymont, outside Wilmington, Delaware, had to travel nearly an hour by bus to Howard High School in Wilmington. Yet white students in Claymont enjoyed

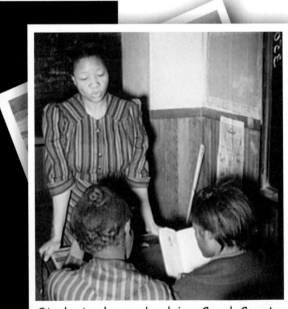

Students share a book in a Creek County, Oklahoma, classroom in 1940.

The Creek County school board provided books to white schools, but black schools had to buy their own. The black schools were overcrowded, and there were not enough books to go around.

a well-equipped school close to their homes that had a variety of courses and afterschool activities. Ethel Belton and seven other African American parents went to Louis Redding, an attorney who had grown up in the area, for help. He told them to ask the State Board of Education to allow their children to attend the school in Claymont, but they were not allowed. As a result, Belton and the parents sued, and the case was tried as *Belton v. Gebhart.*

The other case developed in Hockessin, Delaware, after Sarah Bulah began driving her daughter "two miles to [an] old one-room schoolhouse," while white students took advantage of a modern school.[3] White students were transported to school by bus, but African Americans were not. Sarah Bulah tried to get the local school board to provide transportation for African American students, but they refused. She also turned to Redding, but Redding said he would help only if Bulah would sue for integration rather than transportation. Bulah and her husband agreed, but the other African American families in her community did not agree with integration. They believed African American students would learn best when they were surrounded by people who cared about them and wanted them to succeed. This might have been true, but both Bulah and Belton decided that integration was more important, and in the case *Bulah v. Gebhart*, the court agreed. Delaware's Attorney General Albert Young did not, so he appealed the case. When it was heard in the Supreme Court, it was called *Gebhart v. Belton.*

The NAACP reluctantly took on one case: *Davis v. County School Board of Prince Edward County*. Robert R. Moton High School in Farmville, Virginia, was built to hold 180 students, but 477 students were enrolled by 1950. The school district built leaky tar paper shacks to hold some students, and they even held classes in the auditorium and on buses. The school did not have a gym or cafeteria, while the white high schools did. After the African American adults in Prince Edward County could not convince the school board to build a new school to replace Moton High, the students decided to take action.

Sixteen-year-old Barbara Rose Johns organized a student strike. First, she went to the student leaders at the school to get their support. She managed to get the principal to leave the school for a few hours and had the entire student body meet in the auditorium. Next, she asked the teachers to leave, and then she told the students she "wanted them to go on strike to demand a better school."[4] The students agreed, even though when the principal returned to school, he tried to talk them out of rebelling against the law. Barbara suggested that they carry picket signs or sit at their desks with their books closed, but in the end, the students decided they would not return to school.

The Reverend L. Francis Griffin helped the students write to the NAACP in Richmond, Virginia, for help. Spottswood Robinson III, a lawyer for the NAACP, visited Farmville, planning to talk the students out of striking. When he saw the work Barbara and the other students had accomplished, he changed his mind. Years later, someone asked Barbara if she had been afraid, and she said she was not afraid. Barbara wanted the African American students at her school to get a good education, and she was not afraid to fight for it.

In 1951, Spottswood Robinson filed a lawsuit in Richmond on behalf of 117 high school students who "asked the state of Virginia to abolish its [order] of segregated schools."[5] The NAACP lost the *Davis* case and quickly appealed to the Supreme Court. The Supreme Court had already decided the year before to hear *Brown* and *Briggs v. Clarendon County* at the same time. Later the Court added *Davis v. County School Board of Prince Edward County*, *Gebhart v. Belton*, and *Bolling v. Sharpe*. In *Bolling v. Sharpe*, eleven African American students sued because they wanted to enroll in an all-white junior high school in Washington, D.C., and were denied admission.

The Supreme Court heard the five cases in 1952, but the judges could not reach a decision. They asked the lawyers to re-argue their cases in the fall of 1953. The judges wanted the lawyers to talk more about their cases and how the Fourteenth Amendment related to the desegregation of schools.

Finally, the *Brown v. Board of Education of Topeka, Kansas*, opinion was read on May 17, 1954. The Court ruled that segregated schools were against the law; schools must desegregate. A student could not be denied admission into a school because of his or her race.

After the opinion was read, Justice Earl Warren said the court would hear arguments about how the schools would desegregate. Thurgood Marshall suggested that desegregation begin immediately, but in a decision called *Brown II*, ruled on May 31, 1955, the Court decided that school districts in the South should develop desegregation plans and carry them out "with all deliberate speed."[6] Some school districts—including those in Washington, D.C., Baltimore, St. Louis, and West Virginia—developed integration plans shortly after the *Brown* decision was read, while others delayed desegregation.

More than ten years before the Fourteenth Amendment was accepted by the states, the U.S. Supreme Court ruled that African Americans were not citizens of the United States and could not have the rights and privileges that citizens enjoyed. Since African Americans were not considered citizens, there was little reason for white people to give them good schools. At that time, African Americans were not allowed to participate in democracy by voting or running for public office.

After the Thirteenth Amendment declared the end of slavery, African Americans still faced racism and unequal treatment. Congress passed the Fourteenth Amendment in June of 1866, and it was approved by the states in July of 1868. The amendment has five sections. The second, third, and fourth sections deal with how to handle the Southern states that left the Union before the Civil War, while the fifth section says Congress has the right to make laws that help people apply the Fourteenth Amendment. The first section is the one that was important to the NAACP lawyers' arguments against school segregation.

Section one states that all citizens should be treated equally under the law, that all people born in (or who become citizens of) the United States are citizens of the country and the state in which they live and should have the same rights.

It also says states cannot create laws that limit the rights of any of its citizens or discriminate against a person or a group of people. State laws also must be rational or clear. Finally, it says that citizens must have due process. This means the government must give its citizens a fair trial before taking a citizen's life, liberty, or other possessions.

NAACP leaders (left to right) Henry L. Moon, director of public relations; Roy Wilkins, executive secretary; Herbert Hill, labor secretary; and Thurgood Marshall, special counsel. The NAACP actively recruited members to help fight for issues important to people of color, including the right to attend decent schools and the right to vote.

A young boy watches a mob of people, some carrying American flags, as they march to Central High School in Little Rock, Arkansas, to protest integration in 1959.

Mobs could be dangerous, and often innocent people were attacked. However, they did not keep young people like the Little Rock Nine, the Norfolk 17, or Ruby Bridges from attending previously all-white schools.

Ending Segregation

Desegregating schools was difficult in some states. When African Americans tried to enroll in previously all-white schools, they were met with resistance. Some states operated as if the Supreme Court had never ruled that segregation was unconstitutional. African Americans risked their lives to end school segregation.

Two years after the *Brown* decision was announced, Autherine Lucy was admitted into the University of Alabama. After she arrived on campus, a mob rioted, and the university asked her to stop coming to school for a while because she was in danger. Lucy sued and won the case, but was expelled anyway because she accused the university of using the riots as an excuse to keep her from attending.

Thurgood Marshall and Lucy talked to a reporter, who suggested that some whites thought the NAACP refused to give them enough time to accept African Americans in American society. Marshall replied, "Maybe you can't override prejudice overnight. The Emancipation Proclamation was issued in 1863, 90-odd years ago. I believe in gradualism, but I also believe that 90-odd years is pretty gradual."[1]

Little Rock, Arkansas, was hoping school desegregation would be slow, too. The superintendant of schools, Virgil T. Blossom, developed a plan in 1954 that would allow elementary schools to integrate first, and then secondary schools would slowly follow. White parents did not like this plan, and they let Blossom know it. City buses and universities were desegregated by 1956, and at least seven districts had integrated its schools by 1957. Meanwhile, Blossom revised Little Rock's desegregation plan, allowing a few African American high school students to attend Central High School.

African American students who were interested in attending Central were often recruited by the NAACP, then tested and interviewed by school board members. Some students were persuaded not to attend Central, while others decided not to attend on their own. In the end, nine students were chosen to integrate the school: Minnijean Brown, Elizabeth Eckford, Ernest Green, Thelma Mothershed, Melba Pattillo, Gloria Ray, Terrence Roberts, Jefferson Thomas, and Carlotta Walls.

In August, after the Mothers' League of Central High School met, a lawsuit was filed to prevent integration. The women argued that violence would erupt and people would get hurt. The governor of Arkansas, Orval Faubus, and others, agreed, but the Court did not. School integration would take place on September 4, 1957.

On September 4, when the African American students walked toward the school building, a row of National Guardsmen stood in their way, blocking the entrance. Governor Faubus had ordered the Guardsmen to allow only white students to enter Central. Since an angry mob stood behind the students shouting insults, and the Guardsmen stood in front of them with guns, the students returned home.

On the other side of the building one of the students, Elizabeth Eckford, was alone because she did not know the others had planned to meet and then attempt to enter the school together. With a notebook tucked under her arm and dark sunglasses on, Elizabeth walked toward Central as rioters shouted racial slurs. They chanted, "Two, four, six, eight, we will not integrate."[2] Petrified, Elizabeth sat on a bench at a bus stop, where she was comforted by two men until Grace Lorch, a white lady, boarded a bus with her and took her to her mother.

The African American students did not return to Central until September 23, 1957. Once again Central was surrounded by a mob, but the police escorted the students into the school through a side entrance. When the mob grew, the police helped the students leave the school safely. The mob was so fierce they began to attack African Americans who were not even involved in school desegregation. They threw bricks through the windows of African American people's homes and businesses, and they beat and harassed African American reporters. The level of violence in Little Rock was so high, the students did not attempt to attend school the next day.

Soon after their arrival in Little Rock, they succeeded in dispersing the mob. The paratroopers helped make the school a safer place for African American students.

Paratroopers with bayonets push back the crowd of protesters, which by September 23 had grown to over 1,000 people.

Woodrow Wilson Mann, the mayor of Little Rock, sent a telegram to President Dwight D. Eisenhower, telling him that the "situation is out of control and police cannot disperse the mob. I am pleading to you as President of the United States . . . to provide the necessary federal troops within several hours. Action by you will restore peace and order."[3] On September 24, Eisenhower responded by sending paratroopers of the 101st Airborne Division from Kentucky to Little Rock. He also placed the Arkansas National Guardsmen who had kept the students out of Central under federal control. It became their job to join the paratroopers in helping Central desegregate peacefully.

Many students refused to attend school the next day because they knew the paratroopers would allow the students to enter Central. Despite help from the troops, white students still found ways to harass the students. They poked them with safety pins, sprayed them with ink, and threw them into lockers.

At the end of the school year, on May 27, 1958, Central graduated its first African American student: Ernest Green. Despite this success, whites all

A Little Rock student takes notes from a class that is broadcast over television.

When Governor Faubus closed the schools in Little Rock, students were forced to find other ways to study. Some people moved to other parts of the United States, while others took courses through the mail, on television, and at small colleges.

across the South still tried to stop desegregation. Governor Faubus closed the schools during the 1958–1959 school year, causing children to look for other ways to continue their education. In 1959, Little Rock's schools reopened, and Carlotta Walls and Jefferson Thomas, two of the nine students who helped integrate the school in 1957, returned to Central.

The following year, New Orleans, Louisiana, began school desegregation with its first graders. African American students were tested to determine who would be allowed to attend two white schools: William Frantz Elementary and McDonogh 19 Elementary. Ruby Bridges and five other girls passed the test. Ruby's father did not think she should attend a previously all-white school because it could be dangerous, but her mother believed that a desegregated school would provide her with a better education. After much discussion, Mr. and Mrs. Bridges decided that sending Ruby to William Frantz would help make it possible for all African American children to go to better schools.

When Ruby was five, she attended Johnson Lockett Elementary School, a school for black children. The following year, she would be allowed to attend a white elementary school.

Ruby Bridges and her family moved to New Orleans, Louisiana, when Ruby was four years old.

A federal judge ruled that New Orleans would begin desegregating on November 14, 1960. Ruby and the other five girls could attend all-white schools, but two of the girls' families decided they no longer wanted their daughters to be among the first to integrate. Three of the girls—Leona Tate, Tessie Prevost, and Gail Etienne—were to attend McDonogh 19, while Ruby would be the only African American student attending William Frantz.

The entire nation had seen the resistance to desegregation displayed in Little Rock just three years earlier, so Judge J. Skelly Wright decided to make it difficult for people to stop integration. He asked federal marshals to escort the girls to school. On the first day, four marshals walked up to the school building with Ruby and her mother. Demonstrators old and young threw things and held up picket signs and burned crosses. Ruby saw and heard the mob, but her mother told her to pray for them. Once Ruby and her mother entered the building, they sat in the principal's office the entire day, where Ruby saw

Top left: An all-white school in White Plains, Green County, Georgia, in 1941. Their small class sizes, neat and well-organized classrooms, and current materials gave white schools a better environment in which to learn.

Bottom left: An all-black school in White Plains, Green County, Georgia, in 1941. The shabby buildings and materials made the students feel inferior to, or less important than, whites. Their schools were overcrowded and understaffed.

Below: New York City Mayor Robert Wagner meets the Little Rock Nine in 1958. Front row, from left to right: Minnijean Brown, Elizabeth Eckford, Carlotta Walls, Mayor Wagner, Thelma Mothershed, Gloria Ray; back row: Terrence Roberts, Ernest Green, Melba Pattillo, and Jefferson Thomas.

white parents taking their children back home because she was in the building.

The next day when the marshals escorted Ruby and her mother to school, the mob returned. One person even carried a black doll in a coffin. This frightened Ruby, but she kept moving forward and into the building where she met her teacher, Barbara Henry. Ruby had never had a white teacher before, but she liked Mrs. Henry from the very beginning. Ruby's mother sat in the classroom as Mrs. Henry taught Ruby different subjects. Some white children remained at William Frantz, though they were separated from Ruby. Ruby had to do everything alone or with Mrs. Henry. It was not even safe for Ruby to go outside for recess.

After several days of attending school with Ruby, Mrs. Bridges had to return to work, so Ruby had to go to school alone. Her mother told her she would be safe with the marshals, but if she became frightened she should pray. Ruby recalls, "That was how I started praying on the way to school. The things people yelled at me didn't seem to touch me. Prayer was my protection."[4] Ruby often prayed, "Please, God, try to forgive those people. Because even if they say those bad things, they don't know what they're doing. So You could forgive them, just like You did those folks a long time ago when they said terrible things about You."[5]

Ruby's family had a difficult time, but people in her community and around the world found ways to help her and her family. Dr. Robert Coles, a child psychiatrist, even volunteered to help Ruby sort out her feelings about what was happening to her.

The mob also threatened the parents of white children who continued to attend William Frantz after Ruby enrolled. As the school year wore on, the size of the mob grew smaller and smaller. By June, the loud protests against school integration had quieted.

When Ruby returned to school for second grade, Mrs. Henry was gone, and so was the mob. Ruby remembers, "There were no marshals, no protestors. There were other kids—even some other black students—in my second-grade class. . . . It was almost as if that first year of school integration had never happened. No one talked about it. Everyone seemed to have put that difficult time behind them. After a while, I did the same."[6]

Autherine Juanita Lucy was born on October 5, 1929, in Shiloh, Alabama, to Minnie Hosea Lucy and Milton Cornelius Lucy. After high school, Autherine attended Selma University in Selma, Alabama, and Miles College in Fairfield, Alabama. She graduated from Miles College with a degree in English in 1952 but decided she wanted to get another degree. A few years before the *Brown* decision was announced, she asked the NAACP to help her get admitted into the University of Alabama. Thurgood Marshall, Constance Baker Motley, and Arthur Shores took on the challenge and became her lawyers.

Lucy knew she was smart enough to attend the school, but she also knew that the university might reject her application simply because she was African American. The NAACP lawyers worked on Lucy's case until finally, on June 29, 1955, a court order forced the University of Alabama to view Lucy's application without regard to her race. The following year, Autherine Lucy was admitted to the University of Alabama. When she arrived on campus in February 1956, a mob rioted. Police escorted her to classes on Monday, but angry people still threatened her. The university suspended her three days later. School officials said they asked Lucy to stop coming to school for a while because she was in danger. With the help of NAACP lawyers, Lucy sued the university because her right to attend the school was taken from her. She won the case, but the university expelled her anyway for accusing the university of "acting in support of the white mob."[7]

Lucy moved away from Alabama and found work as a teacher, but during the 1970s she moved back to her home state. More than thirty years passed before the University of Alabama allowed Lucy to attend again. By then, her daughter, Grazia Foster, had decided to attend too. Lucy studied elementary education. She and her daughter graduated from the University of Alabama in 1992. Lucy received a master's degree in elementary education.

Autherine Lucy (left) leaves federal court with her lawyers Thurgood Marshall (center) and Arthur Shores.

A black student walks to Clinton High School in Tennessee after the school was desegregated.

Integrating an all-white school was not an easy task. Many blacks felt they would not be accepted or liked by teachers or students. They also feared being beaten or harassed. To make matters worse, the all-white schools were in areas far away from their own communities.

CHAPTER 4

Desegregation Continues

The fight for school desegregation continued in other places. In Prince Edward County, Virginia, where Barbara Johns had led the student strike at Robert R. Moton High School, the schools were closed from 1959 to 1964 to avoid school desegregation. In 1965, after Virginia's massive resistance ended, New Kent County, Virginia, developed "freedom of choice" plans.[1]

New Kent County had two schools, one for African Americans and one for whites. In an effort to desegregate, the school board offered a plan that allowed "students to choose the school they wished to attend."[2] While some African American students chose to attend the previously all-white school, New Kent, white students did not choose to attend Watkins, the previously all-black school. In 1968, the court ruled in *Green v. New Kent County, Virginia*, that freedom of choice plans were not enough to help achieve integration, as most children were remaining in their original schools. The language used in the ruling suggested that the *Brown* decision required school integration, creating racially balanced schools, rather than desegregation, getting rid of laws that exclude students from schools because of their race. Thus, although many courts use the words *integration* and *desegregation* as if they mean the same thing, they are not the same. When court documents began to use the terms *integration* and *desegregation* interchangeably, or as if they mean the same thing, the NAACP and others turned their attention to segregation in the North and other places.

In 1954, when the *Brown* ruling said segregated schools were unconstitutional, Washington, D.C., and seventeen states—Alabama, Arkansas, Delaware, Florida, Georgia, Kentucky, Louisiana, Maryland, Mississippi, Missouri, North Carolina, Oklahoma, South Carolina, Tennessee, Texas, Virginia, and West Virginia—had laws that upheld segregation. By 1957, only

There were white classmates who welcomed them and made them feel they belonged, even though these white students risked bullying from students who did not like blacks.

While some black students had horrible experiences during the first few years of integration, some formed friendships with whites.

a little over half of the states had begun desegregating their schools. Other states, including Kansas, Massachusetts, and Arizona, may not have had laws that required segregation, but segregation often existed because of residential segregation. Residential segregation occurs when African Americans and whites do not share the same neighborhoods. Since segregation in some form existed in the North and the South, it was clear that segregation was ingrained in American society. Several things happened to help nudge states to desegregate despite residential segregation.

The Civil Rights Act of 1964, which states that segregation is illegal, encouraged school districts to desegregate. Part of the act allowed the Department of Health, Education, and Welfare to find out whether desegregation had been obtained in school districts and, if it had, to what extent. The act also allowed the government to deny federal funding to local school districts that did not meet federal guidelines for integration. Affirmative action, which "sought to desegregate universities and workplaces by encouraging the hiring of blacks," also helped.[3] Shortly after the act was put in place, schools in southern states began integrating.

Charlotte, North Carolina, an urban area where few African Americans and whites shared neighborhoods, had a difficult time integrating its schools. In order to make integration easier, the 1971 Supreme Court ruling of *Swann v. Charlotte-Mecklenburg Board of Education* required the schools to use busing—the act of transporting African American and white students to schools in neighborhoods far from their own to achieve integration.

School districts in large cities in the North shared Charlotte's problem of residential segregation. When whites in a neighborhood near New York City were asked what they felt about the possibility of African Americans moving into their neighborhood, they said things like, "The time is not ripe yet," and "I don't discriminate, but I wouldn't want one [an African American person] as a neighbor."[4] Though other responses—such as, "I don't care; I'm in my

The Equal Employment Opportunity Commission, established three years earlier by President John F. Kennedy, would enforce the Civil Rights Act and other laws that prohibit discrimination.

President Lyndon B. Johnson signs the Civil Rights Act of 1964 before other supporters of the bill, including Martin Luther King Jr.

Throughout his career, Thurgood Marshall helped put an end to segregation in schools and other public places.

In 1967, President Johnson appointed him to the Supreme Court. Justice Marshall continued to support civil rights. He also argued for affirmative action. He served on the Court until his retirement in 1991.

house; they're in theirs"—were more positive, it was clear that it would take time for Northerners to accept residential integration.[5]

In the meantime, the Supreme Court gave the same answer to Northerners that it gave to Southerners: busing. A series of court rulings during the 1970s urged school districts in the North and other areas to integrate and to use busing to accomplish it. For example, in a Supreme Court case involving segregation in Denver, Colorado, busing was mandated.

By 1972, more African American children in the South attended majority white schools than African American students in the North did. To help achieve racial balance in its schools, Detroit's school system wanted to require busing between its schools and schools in surrounding areas. Detroit's school district had mostly African American students in 1970, while the school systems just outside the city had mostly white students. The schools were clearly segregated, but there was no evidence that the schools were segregated because of racism. Some argued that the schools were segregated largely because Detroit had a predominantly African American population, and because many of the white school-age children attended private schools or lived outside Detroit.

A district court judge planned to fix the segregation, so he ordered the Detroit school system and "53 surrounding districts" to become one large district.[6] In the 1974 Supreme Court case *Milliken v. Bradley*, the Supreme Court ruled against integrating predominantly African American schools in Detroit, with schools in the suburbs. Thurgood Marshall, who was the first African American to serve as a Supreme Court Justice, was disappointed and voiced his disagreement with the ruling. He said the Court ruling did not help fight separate and unequal education. He also said, ". . . for unless our children begin to learn together, there is little hope that our people will ever learn to live together."[7]

Though busing was not a new idea in the American educational system, African American and white parents did not want their children to be bused outside their neighborhoods. People who studied busing programs felt busing led to more segregation because large numbers of white students who did not want to participate in integration began attending private schools. Some argued that busing was expensive, while others said it was too time-consuming: Students spent a great deal of time traveling to and from school. Nevertheless, major cities such as Cleveland, Los Angeles, and Louisville continued to have busing programs for years without much resistance.

Some urban cities were not so lucky. In Boston, Massachusetts, where over 100 years earlier Sarah Roberts tried to attend the all-white school near her home, whites fought against busing so passionately, they grew as violent as Southerners did during the Little Rock crisis. The busing plan in Boston required "1,746 nonwhite" students from a predominantly African American neighborhood called Roxbury to be bused to South Boston, a community made up of mostly whites, while over "1,271 white pupils" were bused to Roxbury and other areas.[8] Citizens in Boston were so angry about court-ordered busing, they lashed out and began rioting. After the busing program began, residents of South Boston threw rocks at the buses that brought African American students to their neighborhood schools. They also attacked African Americans who were not a part of the busing program but just happened to be in their neighborhood. Violence occurred in Roxbury too as African American students threw rocks at whites.

Police officers in Boston escort buses to help keep the students safe. People who did not like the idea of students being bused to schools in different parts of Boston often grew violent.

In cities like Chicago, the struggle for school desegregation lasted for years. As in other cities, officials in Chicago took action against desegregation by changing school boundaries so that white children would not have to attend certain schools. Many white families moved to the suburbs, and some enrolled their children in private and parochial schools (schools run by churches). The city finally developed a desegregation plan in 1980, but by that time, integration was difficult to achieve because few whites were enrolled in public schools.

FOR YOUR INFORMATION

Some people argue that affirmative action is about quotas and reverse discrimination. They say people of color and women have an unfair advantage when seeking jobs and school admissions. If this is true, why does the United States have an affirmative action policy?

Before affirmative action had a name and a function, the United States had passed several amendments it hoped would help bring equality to all Americans. Two of the amendments, the Thirteenth, which declared the end of slavery, and the Fourteenth, which says all United States citizens are protected equally under the law, were passed during Reconstruction. Twenty years later, blacks still faced discrimination. In fact, court rulings made segregated hospitals, jails, schools, and so on the way of life in the South.

Along with segregation came the attitude that blacks were inferior to whites. Most blacks were forced to take lower-paying jobs as maids and chauffeurs, and they had fewer opportunities to attend universities. Even when blacks enlisted in the military, most were laborers, not trained fighters. Black leaders spoke out. In 1941, A. Philip Randolph told President Franklin D. Roosevelt that 100,000 blacks would march on Washington if he did not do something to help blacks get the opportunity to compete for better jobs. Under pressure, President Roosevelt signed Executive Order 8802. The order said government employers would not discriminate against applicants because of their "race, creed, color, or national origins."[9] The order did little to reduce discrimination.

Over the years, the government continued to pass laws designed to stop racism, but it continued. In 1961, President John F. Kennedy introduced Executive Order 10925 on television. The order said the President's Committee on Equal Employment Opportunity would "take affirmative action to ensure that applicants are employed, and that employees are treated . . . without regard to their race, creed, color, or national origin."[10] It would take the civil rights movement and firm enforcement of affirmative action to convince employers and schools to admit people without regard to their race or gender. Some argue that without affirmative action, United States schools and places of employment might not be as diverse as they are today.

Affirmative action has helped companies achieve a diverse workforce—and workers a chance to hold jobs that otherwise might have been closed to them.

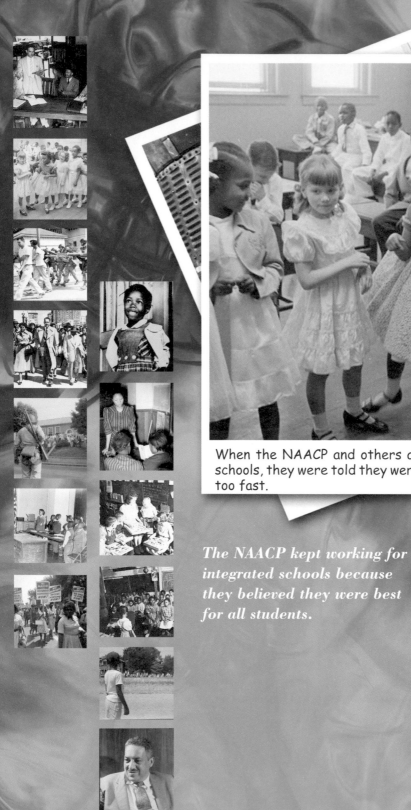

When the NAACP and others argued for integrated schools, they were told they were asking for too much, too fast.

The NAACP kept working for integrated schools because they believed they were best for all students.

Desegregation Now

"We conclude that in the field of public education the doctrine of 'separate but equal' has no place. Separate educational facilities are . . . unequal," the Supreme Court said in *Brown v. Board of Education of Topeka, Kansas*.[1] It has been over fifty years since the Brown decision was read, yet segregation in schools in the United States still exists. Since the 1970s, the South boasted that it had more desegregated schools than the North, but this has changed. By 2009, school systems that were desegregated in the South and the North had started to become segregated. Scholars call this resegregation. A number of circumstances have contributed to resegregation.

Several presidents did not promote school desegregation. President Richard Nixon disagreed with the Supreme Court when it decided that busing should be used to achieve school integration, and he tried to get Congress to end busing. President Nixon did not support busing for several reasons. For example, he did not want to anger southern voters. He also believed busing was the wrong approach to take, and he believed it would weaken neighborhood schools. Unsuccessful, Nixon chose four judges to serve on the Supreme Court that he believed shared his views about desegregation and civil rights. It was during Nixon's term that the Supreme Court decided "the Constitution requires desegregation but not integration as such."[2] The Supreme Court also said local control of schools is important. Thus, suburban school districts around Detroit, Michigan—largely made up of whites—were not required to integrate with schools in Detroit. The Supreme Court ruled that schools had certain boundaries or attendance areas that must be respected. As a result, many school districts did not try to desegregate. Instead, they focused on improving neighborhood schools.

It was also during Nixon's term as president that people began to wonder if equal education meant that all students should go to schools that receive equal amounts of funding. Schools in poor and working-class neighborhoods had less money and resources than schools in wealthy neighborhoods, but the Supreme Court decided against requiring "equal statewide . . . funding."[3]

School desegregation has been successful in some ways. Colleges and universities usually accept qualified African American applicants without the violence and cruelty that Autherine Lucy and others experienced when they tried to attend white colleges and universities in the 1950s and 1960s. Affirmative action has helped ensure that some African Americans and people from other groups (such as Asian Americans, Native Americans, and women) receive the opportunity to attend college. While affirmative action seemed to be successful, it is often viewed as a way to discriminate against whites.

In the 1970s, Allan Bakke sued the University of California at Davis twice for denying him admission into its medical school because he was white.[4] In 1978, the Supreme Court sided with Bakke. It ruled that he be admitted to

Allan Bakke graduates from the University of California Medical School in 1982 after winning a case that challenged affirmative action.

Affirmative action was an effort to create racial balance in schools and places of employment. In the Bakke case, the courts ruled that race is only one factor that can be considered when schools are admitting students; it cannot be the only factor.

the school. Since then, other cases about university admissions to schools have challenged the fairness of affirmative action.

Under President Ronald Reagan's leadership in the 1980s, according to Kluger, "the U.S. government . . . pronounced desegregation a failure, not to mention costly and unpopular."[5] Even though some U.S. citizens disagreed, it was clear that desegregation was no longer a goal. By the end of President Reagan's term, court supervision of school desegregation plans decreased. They were reduced even further during the early 1990s when George H. W. Bush served as U.S. president.

After Thurgood Marshall retired from the Supreme Court in 1991, several important rulings helped encourage resegregation. Between 1992 and 1995, the Supreme Court decided that desegregation programs were not meant to be followed forever. School districts began to end desegregation programs and focused on improving neighborhood schools. Court orders even forced areas such as Denver, Colorado; Charlotte, North Carolina; and Kansas City, Missouri, which were important in the struggle for desegregation, to end their desegregation plans. The Court also said that race could not be used as a reason for assigning a student to a school.

Some say schools are more segregated today than they were in 1954 when the Supreme Court ruled that schools had to desegregate. When schools began to desegregate, many whites decided to take their children out of public schools. This has contributed to resegregation, because public schools in some areas have few whites attending them, so it is nearly impossible to have a racially balanced, or integrated, student body.

When the nation celebrated the 50th anniversary of the integration of Central High School in Little Rock, Arkansas, white and African American teachers and students at Central were working side by side. Desegregation seemed to be successful there. The school even had an African American student body president. But the teachers and the principal noticed that segregation took different forms. The principal, Nancy Rousseau, tried to convince the students to participate in "Mix-up Day," a program she hoped would encourage students of different races to sit together at lunch.[6] When she looked around at lunchtime, she found many students had decided to ignore the idea of sitting with someone of a different race. Instead, they sat with their friends, who in most cases appeared to be people who shared their race.

Unlike most of the white students at Central, many of the African American students were poor. More than fifty years after *Brown*, the neighborhood around the school had boarded-up and abandoned buildings. In 2007, as Little Rock, Arkansas, celebrated Martin Luther King Jr.'s birthday, Mayor Mark Stodola said, "I think Dr. Martin Luther King, Jr. would be . . . disappointed in looking around the neighborhoods of Central High . . . looking at what we have not accomplished yet in terms of a community. . . . I hope I can help in some way to rid ourselves of those elements of segregation."[7]

Schools are also segregated academically. There are few African American and Latino students at Central or at other high schools in the country enrolled in the advanced courses that prepare students for college. More whites are placed in gifted and talented programs, while African Americans and Latinos outnumber whites in special education classrooms.

Many in the country have looked back and noticed that school desegregation had costs. Before the *Brown* case, people within the African American community disagreed about whether integrating schools was more important than fighting for equal funding and resources for all-black schools. Today, some African Americans still disagree. A number of all-black schools were seen as historical landmarks to African Americans, but some were destroyed or closed after schools desegregated. When schools integrated, black communities and educators lost as well as gained. According to Walter G. Stephan's book, "Over 1,000 black educators lost their jobs between 1968 and 1971. During the same period, more than 5,000 white educators were hired."[8] Andrew Heidelberg, one of the Norfolk 17 who integrated schools in Norfolk, Virginia, said, "Ours [black schools] were always years behind, but we actually had the best teachers because they taught us with love and care. They were dedicated to us. That's what went out the window when integration came."[9] Most all-black schools taught children the contributions of African Americans past and present, but it took years before integrated schools began to teach the histories of other cultural groups.

Desegregating schools has always been difficult work. Patricia Turner, another of the Norfolk 17, said, "Becoming the Norfolk 17 was not an easy job."[10] But it was an important job that helped make better schools available for students. School officials say they are committed to providing quality education for all. If resegregation continues, hopefully they will continue to do so.

In 1958, J. Lindsay Almond Jr., the governor of Virginia, closed schools in Richmond, Charlottesville, and Norfolk to avoid desegregation. In 1956, Virginia's government officials refused to provide funding for school districts that tried to integrate, yet whites received money to open private schools. By 1957, Judge Walter E. Hoffman ruled that the schools in Virginia must integrate, but the state tried to ignore the ruling.

When 151 African American students applied to go to all-white schools in Norfolk, they were denied admission. Once again, Judge Hoffman explained that Virginia's schools had to desegregate, so the Norfolk school district agreed to admit 17 of the 151 applicants. These 17 students were assigned to different schools: Andrew Heidelberg, Delores Johnson, Alveraze Frederick Gonsouland, Johnnie Rouse, Olivia Driver, Carol Wellington, and Patricia Godbolt were assigned to Norview High; Louis Cousins to Maury High; Betty Jean Reed to Granby High; Geraldine Talley to Northside Jr. High; Lolita Portis and Reginald Young to Blair Jr. High; and Edward Jordan, LaVera Forbes, Patricia Turner, James Turner Jr., and Claudia Wellington to Norview Jr. High.

Johnnie Rouse points to a photo of her in 1959, when she was one of the Norfolk 17. At the February 2, 2009, event, Governor Tim Kaine apologized for the state's actions fifty years before and unveiled markers that would commemorate the Norfolk 17.

When the students tried to begin school in September 1958, the school board refused to open the schools. Governor Almond eventually took them over. He left six closed, removing them from the public school system.[11] Virginians tried to convince him to reopen the schools, but he refused.

In Norfolk, Virginia, 10,000 students were shut out of schools because of Virginia's massive resistance to school desegregation. However, the all-black schools remained open—though the Norfolk 17 were taught at the First Baptist Church Norfolk. One of the students, Andrew Heidelberg, said, "Man, they busted our butts in that church school. . . . They over prepared us for the White schools."[12] Five months later, on February 2, 1959, the schools were finally opened, and the 17 African American students were allowed to enter previously all-white schools.

Like many schools in the United States, Norfolk Public Schools began busing in the 1970s to help integrate its schools, but large numbers of whites left the school system to go to private schools. By 2001, the district had ended its busing programs, and resegregation began.

Chronology

1850   In *Sarah C. Roberts v. The City of Boston*, Chief Justice Lemuel Shaw states that segregated schools are legal.

1865   The Freedmen's Bureau is established. The Thirteenth Amendment says slavery is illegal.

1868   The Fourteenth Amendment secures citizenship rights for every American, including African Americans.

1896   The Supreme Court supports the decision of *Plessy v. Ferguson*, which states that separate but equal facilities for blacks and whites are legal.

1940   The National Association for the Advancement of Colored People (NAACP) establishes its Legal Defense and Educational Fund.

1951   Barbara Rose Johns leads a student strike at Robert R. Moton High School in Prince Edward County, Virginia.

1954   In *Brown v. Board of Education of Topeka, Kansas*, the Supreme Court says schools in the United States should be desegregated.

1955   In *Brown II*, ruled on May 31, the Court says school districts in the South should develop desegregation plans and carry them out "with all deliberate speed."

1956   Autherine Lucy is admitted to the University of Alabama.

1957   Nine students integrate Little Rock, Arkansas's, Central High School.

1958   Central High School graduates its first African American student: Ernest Green. Norfolk Public Schools are under the control of Governor J. Lindsay Almond Jr.

1959   Prince Edward County, Virginia, closes its schools to avoid desegregation. The Norfolk 17 attend previously all-white schools.

1960   Ruby Bridges is one of the students chosen to integrate schools in New Orleans, Louisiana.

1964   President Lyndon B. Johnson signs the Civil Rights Act of 1964.

Chronology

1968 In *Green v. New Kent County, Virginia*, the Court rules that freedom of choice plans are not enough to help achieve integration.

1971 The Supreme Court ruling in *Swann v. Charlotte-Mecklenburg Board of Education* says school districts should use busing to help integrate the schools.

1974 Citizens of Boston, Massachusetts, respond violently to court-ordered busing.

1986 The Supreme Court says the school districts that have integrated no longer have to use desegregation plans.

1995 The Supreme Court says school districts can have local control of schools.

2001 The Civil Rights Project at Harvard University finds that schools are resegregating.

2004 The 50th anniversary of *Brown v. Board of Education of Topeka, Kansas* is celebrated.

2007 The 50th anniversary of school integration at Central High School in Little Rock, Arkansas, is celebrated.

2008 A memorial honoring Virginian civil rights activists, including Barbara Rose Johns, is dedicated.

2009 In light of the inauguration of African American president Barack Obama, Gary Orfield of the Civil Rights Project comments, "It would be a tragedy if the country assumed from the Obama election that the problems of race have been solved, when many inequalities are actually deepening. The lesson to take from this is that we have elected a brilliant president, who is the product of excellent integrated schools and colleges. We should work hard to extend such opportunities to and develop the talents of the millions of blacks and Latinos who still face isolation and denial of an equal chance."*

* "Press Release: School Resegregation and Civil Rights Challenges for the Obama Administration: A New Report from the Civil Rights Project at UCLA," January 14, 2009

Timeline in History

1861   The Civil War begins.

1863   Lincoln's Emancipation Proclamation ends slavery in the United States of America.

1865   The Civil War ends.

1876   Reconstruction ends.

1909   The National Association for the Advancement of Colored People (NAACP) is founded.

1929   Civil rights leader Dr. Martin Luther King Jr. is born.

1947   Jackie Robinson becomes the first African American player in Major League Baseball.

1955   Montgomery Bus Boycott begins in Montgomery, Alabama.

1961   The Freedom Riders travel south to help end discrimination on buses.

1962   James Meredith, the first African American student to enroll in the University of Mississippi, is escorted to class by U.S. Marshals.

1963   Dr. King gives his "I Have a Dream" speech at the March on Washington for Jobs and Freedom in Washington, D.C.

1967   Thurgood Marshall becomes the first African American Supreme Court Justice.

1968   Richard Milhous Nixon is elected president of the United States.

1973   Tom Bradley becomes the first African American mayor of Los Angeles, California.

1989   Autherine Lucy enrolls in the University of Alabama to get a master's degree in elementary education.

1990   Douglas Wilder becomes the governor of Virginia. He is the first African American to be elected governor in the United States.

1991   Clarence Thomas becomes the second African American Supreme Court Justice.

2009   Barack Obama becomes the first African American U.S. president. Michael Steele becomes the first African American Republican National Committee Chairman.

Chapter Notes

Chapter 1. Separate and Unequal
1. Henry Hampton and Judith Vecchione, *Eyes on the Prize: Fighting Back, 1957–1962*, DVD (Alexandria, VA: PBS, 2006).

Chapter 2. *Brown v. Board of Education of Topeka, Kansas*
1. Walter G. Stephan, "A Brief Historical Overview of School Desegregation," in *School Desegregation: Past, Present, and Future*, ed. Walter G. Stephan and Joe R. Feagin (New York: Plenum Press, 1980), p. 11.
2. Richard Kluger, *Simple Justice: The History of Brown v. Board of Education and Black America's Struggle for Equality* (New York: Vintage, 2004), p. 409.
3. Kluger, p. 435.
4. Juan Williams, *Eyes on the Prize: America's Civil Rights Years, 1954–1965* (New York: Viking, 1987), p. 25.
5. Williams, p. 27.
6. Lino A. Graglia, "From Prohibiting Segregation to Requiring Integration: Developments in the Law of Race and the Schools since Brown," in *School Desegregation: Past, Present, and Future*, ed. Walter G. Stephan and Joe R. Feagin (New York: Plenum Press, 1980), p. 72.

Chapter 3. Ending Segregation
1. Henry Hampton and Judith Vecchione, *Eyes on the Prize: Fighting Back, 1957-1962*, DVD (Alexandria, VA: PBS, 2006).
2. Ibid.
3. Dwight D. Eisenhower Presidential Library and Museum: "Western Union Telegram from Mayor Woodrow Wilson Mann," http://www.eisenhower.archives.gov/dl/LittleRock/amManntoPresident92457pg1.pdf.
4. Ruby Bridges, "The Story," http://www.rubybridges.com/story.htm.
5. Robert Coles, *The Story of Ruby Bridges* (New York: Scholastic, 1995), n.p.
6. Ruby Bridges, "The Story."
7. Darlene Clark Hine, ed., *Black Women in America: An Historical Encyclopedia* (New York: Carlson Publishing, Inc., 1993), p. 448.

Chapter 4. Desegregation Continues
1. Lino A. Graglia, "From Prohibiting Segregation to Requiring Integration: Developments in the Law of Race and the Schools since Brown," in *School Desegregation: Past, Present, and Future*, ed. Walter G. Stephan and Joe R. Feagin (New York: Plenum Press, 1980), p. 77.

2. Ibid., p. 76.
3. Nick Treanor, ed. *Desegregation*, (Farmington Hills, MI: Greenhaven Press, 2003), p. 28.
4. James Peck, "Segregation Exists in the North, Too," in *Desegregation*, ed. by Nick Treanor (Farmington Hills, MI: Greenhaven Press, 2003), p. 165.
5. Ibid.
6. Graglia, pp. 86–87.
7. Richard Kluger, *Simple Justice: The History of Brown v. Board of Education and Black America's Struggle for Equality* (New York: Vintage, 2004), p. 767.
8. Time, "Racial Violence in the North," in *Desegregation*, ed. by Nick Treanor (Farmington Hills, MI: Greenhaven Press, 2003), p. 187.
9. Terry H. Anderson, *The Pursuit of Fairness: A History of Affirmative Action* (New York: Oxford, 2004), p. 22.
10. Ibid., p. 60.

Chapter Five. Desegregation Now
1. Richard Kluger, *Simple Justice: The History of Brown v. Board of Education and Black America's Struggle for Equality* (New York: Vintage, 2004), p. 793.
2. Lino A. Graglia, "From Prohibiting Segregation to Requiring Integration: Developments in the Law of Race and the Schools since Brown," in *School Desegregation: Past, Present, and Future*, ed. Walter G. Stephan and Joe R. Feagin (New York: Plenum Press, 1980), p. 88.
3. Kluger, p. 765.
4. Ibid., p. 774.
5. Ibid., p. 768.
6. Brent Renaud and Craig Renaud, *Little Rock Central: 50 Years Later* DVD (New York: Home Box Office, 2007).
7. Ibid.
8. Walter G. Stephan, "A Brief Historical Overview of School Desegregation," in *School Desegregation: Past, Present, and Future*, ed. Walter G. Stephan and Joe R. Feagin (New York: Plenum Press, 1980), p. 19.
9. Wil LaVeist, "Homecoming for Norfolk 17," *Mix Magazine*, July 2008, p. 12.
10. Amy Couteé, "Woman Vividly Recalls School Desegregation as Part of Norfolk 17," *The Virginian-Pilot*, February 25, 2008, p. 3.
11. Old Dominion University, "School Desegregation in Norfolk Virginia," http://www.lib.odu.edu/special/schooldesegregation/.
12. LaVeist, p. 10.

Further Reading

For Young Adults

Fradin, Judith Bloom, and Dennis Brindell Fradin. *The Power of One: Daisy Bates and the Little Rock Nine*. New York: Clarion, 2004.

Haskins, Jim. *Separate, But Not Equal: The Dream and the Struggle*. New York: Scholastic, 1998.

Hudson, David L., Jr. *The Fourteenth Amendment: Equal Protection Under the Law*. Berkeley Heights, NJ: Enslow Publishers, 2002.

Sharp, Anne Wallace. *Separate but Equal: The Desegregation of America's Schools*. Detroit: Lucent Books, 2007.

Works Consulted

Altman, Susan. *The Encyclopedia of African-American Heritage*. New York: Facts on File, Inc., 1997.

Anderson, Terry H. *The Pursuit of Fairness: A History of Affirmative Action*. New York: Oxford, 2004.

Bridges, Ruby. *Through My Eyes*. New York: Scholastic, 1999.

Coles, Robert. *The Story of Ruby Bridges*. New York: Scholastic, 1995.

Couteé, Amy. "Woman Vividly Recalls School Desegregation as Part of Norfolk 17." *The Virginian-Pilot*. February 25, 2008.

Gilbert, Peter. *With All Deliberate Speed: A Look at the Landmark Brown vs. the Board of Education*. DVD. Silver Spring, MD: Discovery Communications, 2004.

Hampton, Henry, and Judith Vecchione. *Eyes on the Prize: Fighting Back, 1957–1962*. DVD. Alexandria, VA: PBS, 2006.

Hine, Darlene Clark, ed. *Black Women in America: An Historical Encyclopedia*. New York: Carlson Publishing, Inc., 1993.

Kendrick, Paul, and Stephen Kendrick. *Sarah's Long Walk: The Free Blacks of Boston and How Their Struggle for Equality Changed America*. Boston, Massachusetts: Beacon, 2004.

Kluger, Richard. *Simple Justice: The History of Brown v. Board of Education and Black America's Struggle for Equality*. New York: Vintage, 2004.

LaVeist, Wil. "Homecoming for Norfolk 17." *Mix Magazine*. July 2008.

Renaud, Brent, and Craig Renaud. *Little Rock Central: 50 Years Later*. DVD. New York: Home Box Office, 2007.

Stephan, Walter G. *School Desegregation: Past, Present, and Future*. New York: Plenum Press, 1980.

Stockley, Grif. *Daisy Bates: Civil Rights Crusader from Arkansas*. Jackson: University of Mississippi Press, 2005.

Treanor, Nick, ed. *Desegregation*. Farmington Hills, MI: Greenhaven Press, 2003.

Walker, Julian. "Memorial Pays Tribute to Those Who Fought School Segregation." *The Virginian-Pilot*, July 22, 2008.

Williams, Juan. *Eyes on the Prize: America's Civil Rights Years, 1954–1965*. New York: Viking, 1987.

On the Internet

The ABCs of School Integration
http://www.tolerance.org/teach/activities/activity.jsp?ar=842&pa=2

Brown v. Board Handbook: *Sarah C. Roberts v. The City of Boston*
http://brownvboard.org/research/handbook/sources/roberts/roberts.htm

Civil Rights 101: School Desegregation and Equal Opportunity
http://www.civilrights.org/research_center/civilrights101/desegregation.html

Dwight D. Eisenhower Presidential Library and Museum: Little Rock School Integration Crisis
http://www.eisenhower.archives.gov/dl/LittleRock/littlerockdocuments.html

NAACP LDF: School Integration
http://www.naacpldf.org/

Old Dominion University: School Desegregation in Norfolk, Virginia
http://www.lib.odu.edu/special/schooldesegregation/

Research: School Desegregation
http://www.civilrightsproject.ucla.edu/research/deseg/reversals_reseg_need.pdf

Robert Russa Moton Museum: Historical Background
http://www.motonmuseum.org

Ruby Bridges: The Story
http://www.rubybridges.com/story.htm

Glossary

abolish (uh-BAH-lish)
To end something that has existed for a long time.

affirmative action (uh-FIR-muh-tiv AK-shun)
A policy designed to remove prejudice when people make decisions about giving women and culturally diverse people opportunities to work and attend schools.

appeal (uh-PEEL)
To ask a court to change a decision made by a lower court.

deliberate (dee-LIH-ber-ayt)
To think about something slowly and carefully before acting.

ingrained (in-GRAYNd)
So much of a habit as to have become part of someone's makeup; describing a habit that is hard to change.

injustice (in-JUS-tiss)
Unfair treatment or reaction.

mandate (MAN-dayt)
Command that something be done.

resistance (ree-ZIS-tunts)
Refusal to accept an idea or situation as it is.

segregation (seh-greh-GAY-shun)
Separating people, usually because of their race.

unconstitutional (un-kon-stih-TOO-shuh-nul)
Not allowed by the U.S. Constitution, the highest law in the land.

PHOTO CREDITS: 34—AP Photo/Peter Bregg; p. 38—AP Photo/Walt Zeboski; p. 41—Office of the Governor of Virginia. All other photos—Library of Congress. Every effort has been made to locate all copyright holders of material used in this book. If any errors or omissions have occurred, corrections will be made in future editions of this book.

Index